GU00802310

contra FLUX

moments caught (*arrested*) whilst in-from motion

Mark Bolsover

First Printing: 2019

ISBN 978-0-244-19086-6

Polyversity Press
Grabenstraße 21/3
8010 Graz
Austria
www.iotacism.com/polyversity

Ineluctable modality of the visible: at least that if no more, thought through my eyes. Signatures of all things I am here to read [. …] *You are walking through it howsomever. I am, a stride at a time. A very short space of time through very short times of space.*

(James Joyce, *Ulysses* [London: Penguin, 1992], p. 45).

Acknowledgments

With thanks to my dear friends Dr Silvia Villa and Dr Christos Hadjiyiannis, and, most of all, to my wife, Jen McGregor, for her continued support..

'the suspension of falling (or,—*Lost Time*)' was originally published in *Mycelia I* (Hedera Felix Press), (Glasgow, October 2018), with thanks to Simone Hutchinson.

'THE SCARLET CAP. (or)—in a climate of paranoid excitation. … ' was originally published in *404 Ink Magazine*, #1 (2016), with thanks to Laura Jones and Heather McDaid.

'UMBRELLA' was originally published in *Pink Cover Zine* (Sydney, September/October 2018), with thanks to Samantha Trayhurn and Ramon Loyola.

'Pokestops—VACUUM. (—in Nikosia).,' was published in *Projectionist's Playground* (December 2018).

Contents

a sign.
—a *message*.
(... —?). ...

on-in (under) an underpass. (—dull, grey non-descript of concrete, and of asphalt). ...

... —(somewhere) on(-along) the Swiss-Italian border. ...

—graffiti.

—a *message*. (*deep*. ... —in its import-connotations.

—an *augury*. ... —?).

...

(—indeed. ...).

9

QUIXOTIC

...

(?)

...

(tall) building. (floors. t' tower. over. (edif)).—gothic (neo). (—*blue-grey* 'v stone(s). ...).
(see face-front. (through the *window*—?).—over-opposite. (street. road).).

(—light. day.—(th') sun's light.—over. onto. ...).

... —*gaps*. (spaces). ... in the soot(-*grime*. dirt. 'v *age* (old) (—dark. grey-*black*(en)-green. *dust*) on-over th' building's front (faç) (grey brick-stone (light).

... —*detail*(s).—statuary (carvings)-ornamenta (ornat). ... —*missing*. (gone).
(—*clean*, *empty* patches(-shapes) (left). ...).

...

—*what if I could **restor**at*? ...

... —would the council let me *have* the building. (buy).—*?*

...—restore, and *expand*. ... —the space-paving. out (-at the) front-side
(—more pave, ... and trees (green(er))? ... —more *space*. and sit (outside)—in the sun's shine (light). ...).

11

...

(inside).

(the building).

(... —dark-low lit. (soft-low.—dull gold-orange(peach-amber)-yellow(-white) (light). ... —lamps (shade). ...). dark wood (mahog)... —floors, and panelled.—tables (round. low). (and chairs). (—a *bar*. (long)). (stools).).

...

the actor.

(has performed).

—a-the show(-the *play*).

...

—three rules (prompts). ...

(*1.*) something good. ... —(?). ... —(?). ...

—t' *improvise* (the scene) (spontane).—fr'm the audience. (called.-suggest). (th' *action*).

...

—th' mountain's top (side). ...

(green. … 'v grass ('n' shrubs-plants-bushels. (*gorse*.—*dark green*)). … —*amber* (orange-(red)-yellow) *faint* 'v sun's set (faint… grey(-white) – lilac 'v the sky (—horizon). …).
…

—Quixote(ic) figure.
(man. (middle-aged?).—long(er) hair. a goatee (beard). …).
(—Caspar Fried- …).

—look out. (over). …

up in the mountain(s).

(to) *alone*.

(—the play). (with the actor). …

…

looking down. the mountain's side (slope(s)).

—into (down) the valley. (narrow. slight).

steep. … grass 'n' gorse (strips-lines 'v bushels).
(*pale* green).

—over (-across). (—th' other *side*…) …

… —sharp. straight. (thin-narrow) spine-pinnac rocks (—mountains' tops(-*peaks*) (—purple-lilac (deep)-*amethyst*…)). rise.
…

…

—been here alone. (here).
(—without *blacklace*).

(for a long time. (*?*)).

(to get away).

…

descent(ding).
(down.—*steep*).

(alone).

(*return*).

…

… —friend (*Jay Arr*).

(as descend)
says—he'd be up for climbing. (back. up. (again)). …
(… —*look back* (up). (—t' th' *peak* (b'hind)).

and *over*… —t' where the thick fog (misted. wet) covers—the
space beyond (above).—the other mountains peaks (—range). …).

—say.—"Then you won't have seen the snow peaks" (beyond)
(in-b'hind the fog. (now). …).

…

snow. (the valley. and the pinnac-peaks.—covered. *cold*. (know).
…).

…

—as round(ing) the valley('s floor.—path-trail). … (—away. path-road). …

rocks. (*huge*).—'t the base(s) 'v the pinnacs… —*broken*.—by th' weight 'v the cold(-snow(s)). …

break.

…

—avalanche(ing). …

fall.—c'llapse. behind us. (the *group*). (—*t'ward* us. *falling.* … —in a *wave* (collapse). …).
(… —*huge*. … —sound (ear-split)-***crack***(s) (*reverb* …), 'v stone-rock(s) (faces). (concuss). …).

—*run.*
(or else we'll be crushed).

…

CURSED(?)
(Trastevere)

(*broad*, but… shadowed-shaded… (—cool-gloomed, … —quiet, 'spite th' moves(ment). … … —*early morning* in-f' the city (the quarter-neighbour-)… (—just beginning (wake)). …).

… —main(?) pedestrian street(-drag). (—*out*. … —into the city('s centre (*heart* 'v)…)—*light* (and traffic (more) at the end of) (—sun-).—the *Tiber* (-bridge). …).

…

—*off*. (there—). …

—t'-in the-that *side's street*. (—on the corner). …

—simply sprayed-written.—on a (—*smooth*-sharp angled(ular),—neo-class., grey-ochre, (—a *corner*. (angles-lines 'v the streets meet)) stone.

…

CURSE

SE QUESTO AMORE (—"IF THIS LOVE" …).
(Trastevere)

…

… —'long. *gloom*-shaded shadow (*cool* (—morning). … —blue-*grey* (slate)) 'v the side's street (cobbled-paved-pedest).

…

(*look* …) …

—*over*. (…)

… —in the-that alley's(way)-*narrow*. (… —functional-municip (obvious) … —f'r the café's-bars-restaurants. (off the main street's drag. …). (bins-refuse)…). …

(… —on torn(-broken-crumbling) wall's plaster. (brick(s)-stone *exposed*. …)

—

—SE QUESTO AMORE E' UNA STORIA E' UNA FAVOLA
...

—(ask) *blacklace* (—trans.)—*what does it mean?* ...

... —*"IF THIS LOVE WERE A STORY, IT WOULD BE A FAIRYTALE".* ...
(—*if* **this** *love were a story.* ...).

(—a *story.* ... —? ...).

...

—not (neither (one 'v us)) *sure*—of the ***tone***.

... —

... —a *serenade*- **love – poem.** (... —? ...).
(... —*livin' the **dream***. (of love).
(a *boast*). ...).

...

or, ...

—a... —*plaint*(?). ...

—a ***protest*** (—angry, *bitter*-sarcastic).
(... —'gainst the *substance* of the love (—love's *lack* of substance). ...

—the (dismal) *fantasy* of a-the relationship ...).
(*aching*-heartbroken... (—?)).

—?

...

an enquiry…
(Trastevere)

—'long the side street. …
(—skirts(skirting)—concrete-mortar-plaster… —later than the
building. …)—by a grating's (grey)-*vent*. …).

…

—line fr'm a song (corrupted)
(—in English. …).
(—in black paint.—(free-)written-sprayed (graffito-*tagged*)). …

…

…

—REGARDING MY *WONDERWALL*. …
(—wall 'v *wonder*. … —with *cryptic*(hieroglyph) (indeciph) its
messages left-sprayed. …).

…

the problem of light pollution
(—fragments from-of a dream).

...

discussing. talk.—about a(-the) play (—production). ...

with friends ('v-fr'm school. ... —*S.* 'n' *A.* (... —still young. ...
)), and singer-actor-director
(—young woman. ... large-square features(-face), (large eyes),
blonde(dark) hair,—pulled back (slight) in-to a tight pony tail. ...
).

in-at a-the restaurant (busy-crowded.—family).

—large space (—*open*). ... —bright-well lit. pale yellow
(walls).—benches–tables (dark wood).—in a booth (benches.—
table (top).—th' middle 'v the room-floor... —t'ward the back. ...
).

—for friends to support (-invest).

...

—the play. ...

—(in) winter (set). (—snow. ... —*real*. ... —wets the audience(s),
at-t' the fringes-wings). ...

—*dark*. ... —Russia(n)—historic. ... —Marxist-socialist (class
(working-lower)) themes. (—actors-cast (—old woman (shawl-
scarved). young men. ...)—in poor worker's dress (stereotyp). ...

—a house (entire.—huge con-struct. dark (black–grey-blue)—
carica-cartoon-itur-ish (*style*).—th'-outside of windows (square-
framed-four pained)—*glow* (... —deep *yellow*). ...

—opens up. …

…

friends're—sceptical (of product).—actor-singer *likes*. …
(—making (hard, determinat) case for. …

—for an essay-thesis).

…

—outside.—the street.
(in the street. … —outside the rest'rant.

—me and *S.* …).

…

dark.—night.—strange, drab (—rough), … c'mmercial part(-area)
'v the city
(… —(pebble-dashed) concrete—grey-beige. shops (small.
business)-restaurants. towers (blocks), and *construction* (sites)…
—over the road(-street) (—busy). …).

…

on a-the corner. (—left.—opposite)… —the theatre. …
(… —see the house… —up-*over* (concrete-dashed) wall (—slabs
'v concrete. rough, grey).

… —see the set. … —***extend*** (—*rise*) out (—up).—fr'm the
theatre-house roof. …

… —cylindric (thick) *tubes*(-sections), in-from 'v the (house's)
structure… —*rise up* (telescope) (… —*huge tower(s)*)-extend,…
—in-t' th' night's sky. …
(looks like will *topple* (fall). …

—leans(-leaning) (over) tower (—'v sections-tubes)
(concertine)…

but,… —*holds* (stands). …).

…

—and move. … —up (along) the street (a-ways).

—t' see. better.

…

—"It *is* impressive." (—*S.*). …

23

(… —continue(s) t' extend (up-out-away)… —up (*curves*-loops around …) (in) the night's sky. …).

—"A full scale (set) *reboot*" (—production), she says. …

…

and I say— …

—"C'n see the Milky Way". …

(—full *belt* (vast) 'v.—*strong*-clear. (*intense* present). … —in-depsite 'v (…—no? …) light pollutes. (—the city's centre). …

—extends up—thick belt-arc(curve)… —fr'm the horizon (—behind (there) streets 'n' buildings)… —up (over).—into the night's sky…

—*vast*. …

—**sublime**. (*awe*. … —aches-quakes—*cool*-electric (—*empty*-hollow *thrill* (tense))—in-through th' stomach-gut's (the *pit*),—up-into in-through the neck's root-base (—spin-al). …).

in-on (—*against*) the (night) sky. …

(—a nebula-ous).

…

—tower (now)—*towers* (on). … —arc-ing (curve)-*loops*… —be-afore the nebulous Way (light 'n' *dust* 'v).
(—extending).

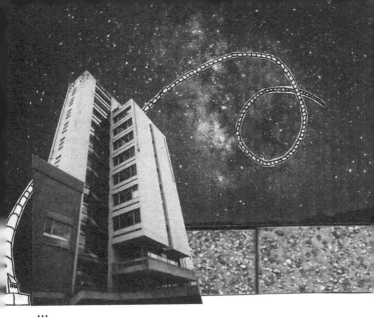

...

—*incredible*.
(... —h've never *seen* (with eyes-own) b'fore. ...).
(... —*rise* (—**drop**). in the stomch-gut's floor (pit.—the base).
(hollow trembling ache (light)-electric).

incomprehens.

excited—*elate*.
(—ache-fizz (slight) buzz (electric),—in the mind-head. ... —
(want-*need*) t' *capture* (—the image-sight,... —the feeling. ...)).

...

and *run*. ... —down the street. (elate).
(—the nebulous is *everywhere* (consume) (in) the (*huge*. .... —
open. ...) sky (night). ...).

and jump—*leap* (in-t' the air). ... —and *float* (—hover (borne up)—*fly*? ...).

and land. (at will).

and jump (—t' leap) again. ... —over the street-road's corner (junction) (before the rest-),... —and *over a car* (still slow-stopping at)...

—*danger*(ous),... but don't care (—know can—will be safe—leaping. ...).

...

back.—into the rest-. (—t' fetch (-collect) (back) my notebook (black (hard)bound...) (—*write down.* ...).

THE BLACK DEVIL!

...

(*Haslach.* ...

—down.—through *The Black Forest* (—*Schwarzwald*). (from
Baden Baden). ... —winter (depth 'v). ... —beautiful (historic-
preserve) (south) German houses-buildings
(... —*European* style... —clean white (painted) houses, slope
(large-steep), terracotta, slate-tile rooves, windows wooden
shuttered (pastel colours painted). ... —in clustered. ...).

—forrest (Black). ... —dense (dark) wooded rich pines (*tall-
thin.*—and small glade-spaces...).—dark (blue-)green. ... —*all*...
dusted (capped) (thick) with snow
(... —light so clean, clear, and *bright* (rich) reflects-refracts off (-
fr'm within) (—forget the *quality*, and intensity of, sometimes)...
).

blank (soft) white-grey (light) 'v the sky. ...

mist... —'v (low) cloud, and 'v steam-mist 'v snow-evaporat (—
light white, thin clouds (-tendril-threads), lines 'v, drift (slow) on-
over hillsides (—steep-sheer, wooded). ...

—past the (steady-fast) rush 'v the train (—*oblong* frame (faint
reflects (light) 'v window). ...).

...

—Black Devils. (—*1969*). ...

... —a sign. (—'bove the door.—side 'v a... shed-like (—industrial). ... —a *bar*.—dark. the rail's side. ...).
BLACK STATION

...

—"BIKERS WELCOME!"

...

—b'neath (—the sign). ...

...

—pedal bikes. ...
(—neat row-line 'v.—locked neat to-on a rail(ing). ... —clean.—bright(-neon) coloured. ... —orderly. ...).

...

(... —solitary (small, smart) silver moped. ...).

...

young, spotty lad—clean-cut (neat hair) (—a teen-student)... (—jeans. a brown-green anorak-a puffer jack- (water proof). ...).

—quietly unlocks his pedal bike.

...

—*__THE BLACK DEVIL!__* …

the suspension of falling.
(or,—*Lost Time*). ...

...

places. (... a house—ruineds—the (open) country(side) (be-aside
the (broad, large, empty) road.—the bottom of a hill's side). ...

—" ... significant for (in-to) Scottish-Scotland's *history*." (... "—
where *the rebel* lived-stayed. ... " ...).

...

—(in-*on*) pages. (large-gloss). 'v a book.—turn(ing). ...

—(as) image(s)-pictures (photo-graphs).

...

ruins.—on-at th' hillside's foot (base.—here...). ... —being
rebuilt (*restor*) (... —red brick structure(s)—ske-*le*tal, ... —
mimic(s) *shapes* 'v all that's left 'v dry (grey-rough) stone ruins
(shapes). ... t' be... —*re-clad* (after) with th' drystone.
(—***shore up***. ... —*preserve*). ...).

(walk(ing).—past).

...

in(to)—(a) cave-cavern (vaulted) (above-over). ... dark(ness)—
up. ...

with *blacklace*.

...

—*things* (-objects), and... *people.* ... —***suspend(ed)***. ... —(and) *hang* (down).—in the darkness (air.—space. (vault). ...).
(... —Nineteenth Cent.(?)—an *armchair* (—light,—beige-grey (rough mat-, coarse),—patterned (dark coloured),... —hangs over (above). ...

(... —)

—man. (white.—middle-aged?). ... —short (neat) dark (black) hair.—(see) back 'v head, and neck (—broken... —? ...).

(... —)

—white, angular (50s Americ)—a convertible. ... —young (little) girl in... —blonde. ...

(... —)

... —*fragments.* ... —'v furnish (wood. (—a banister). ... —'v rock (debris-dross). ...).

...

—the (bed) rock b'neath the town on (*top* 'v) the hill. ... — collapsed (beneath. under mined.—the cavern. ...), and the town (... —insides (only-lone) 'v all the houses-build), and the people (town's folk) (unaware—unsuspect-incomprehend)... —*fell*. (—down.—in-t' the dark. ('v the cavern). ...).

...

—a hundred (—more) years agone. ...
(—(become) a tourist's—*attraction*. (... —?). ...).

...

31

and hang (still—'til now. (this time).). …

…

—suspend(ed).—in a bubble (spher),—of *slow-slowed time*
(distort-distend—suspended).
(… —formed in (the wake 'v) the *moment* 'v the fall-collapse. …

—doesn't affect us (—outwith) (—after the moment of the fall).
…).

…

—*not* stopped-halted. (full—arrest. …).

…

time still—*moves* (… —on-for-onwards). … —infinitesimal
slow-ly (—motion. … —impercept. …).

…

—falling for centuries. (*without* falling. … —without dying-end).

…

with *blacklace*.
(cave's floor. … —'mongst the rocks. …).

…

—worry.—that-'bout th' safety 'neath the fall-suspended ruin-
fragments (falling).

(pull her aside).

…

… —as things-fragments-people-*bodies* reach near the cave's floor (… —few-a coupl'-a feet)… —time, for the fragments-bodies,… —'celarates. (… —c'n *see*. …).

—the sphere's (—a force field-bubble—shimmers (vis)) end.

…

—and (all)… —*re-enters* time's flow. (as for us).

…

but the bubble ('v slow-time slowed), … —kills (softens-arrests-dampens) all their *momentum*.

—drop quiet.

…

… —not the fall of the town (as happened-was)… —only (a) fall of a few feet.

…

…—and the first t' *leave* (—t' *exit*) the bubble, … —*drop* (land).
…
(… —we're the first (only) t' *witness* (anyone-thing leave—t' exit). …
(—t' the cave's floor).

(… —bodies—*cold* (fr'm ages suspended). (clammy). … —shocked by fall, but un-comprehend-aware (—'v the bubble-sphere… —'v the ages past. …).

33

…

—the young girl. …

—approaches with a knife (blade.—sharp-thin) (—fr'm the ruins-rubble fallen).

—swinging. …

(—cuts my arm). …

(—not her fault (blame). …).—she's shocked (trauma) (by-fr'm the fall), and so *angry*. …

—"*How long will I have to be back?!*" …

THE SCARLET CAP.
(or)—in a climate of paranoid excitation. …

…

café… space (—a… *concourse*? open.—central. (*exposed?*).—
bland, pastel, plastic (tables 'n' chairs (angular)). …).

strange. … —t' have people—busied-rushed, and *focussed*—mill-
flowing (—a dull *surge*) past (round), as y' try t' sit, quiet, relaxed
(*try*) amidst, and eat this… —slightly *damp,*—*compressed* 'n' sad
(grey) sandwich (flavourless, in th' main)—(hugely) over-priced,
and t' drink this bitter, flat coffee. …
(a victim, then, (again, no doubt), of th' *captive market* economics
o' these places. …).

… —rush-surging (pulse-es) by,… —through t' th' gates
(departures).

—(the departures) *lounge* (loung-*es*). …

flights.

…

sat.—across, here.—from that drab, commercial (airport. captive)
bookshop (over). …

…

—man.

in a red (—a *scarlet*) cap.
(… —*odd*... —?)

(… perhaps in the wake (so to) of *all* those recent (and not so recent now) *events*… —*attacks*. (Iraq, Belgium, Paris…)… —th' world over… and in this… *ongoing*, … *pervasive*, and longer… *climate*(-atmosphere) of (—*heightened*) paranoid fear (anxiet). …).

…

man in the red cap. …

—large, grey, heavy(-looking) grey parker jacket (coat). (*too* heavy f' th' time-season… —? … —pockets… —*noticeably*— suspiciously—*stuffed* (—bulge.—full). …

(young-ish). unshaven (rough-rugged).—*sallow*? baggy (slight), 'n' tattered jeans. …

… —*hanging around* (so to). … —loiter(-loitering)-lingers in the broad, open entrance of the book store (in front).
(…

—something in… demeanour (yes)-his *stance* (—his *bearing*). … —a nerv-self-consc.(aware) discomfort (tense, slight). … —*awkwardness*. …).

—doesn't go in. (—*?*).

—*goes* in.

—looks (browses, inattent) at books.—*distracted* (?—a *show* of browsing—perform)… —not *really* looking (paying attent). … … —the *act* (action—pretence) in-of browsing (—the "*browse*" …)… —an attempt (*failed*-failing)—t' look "*natural*"-casual. (… —the act, ironic, serves to *betray*, and t' *highlight* his nervs-awkward (self-consc.). …).

(—what *is* under his coat—grey (tee-) shirt? …

—no obvious objects-lumps ('n'-or bumps)… —only a slight paunch (slight). …).

—*does he* mean ill (intent)—? …
(why pretend-ing t' hang around (nerv-obvious self-consc.)—?).

(*watch*.—with (half-) *genuine* nerv-concern. (nerv accelerat (cool, hollow rush-rise) in the chest(-heart) felt. *buzz* (electric) slight sharpen in muscle-sinews (arms). tense in the head(-mind). …).

(—entertain half-fantasy visions (semi-involunt) (*play*.—over 'n' over)… —of explosion (sudden (deafening?) burst-roar—deep-heavy concussion (gravitat)).

heat. 'n' flame (—a *wave*)…

—sounding the alarm… —"*DOWN!*" (—see it coming, prompt-ed by astute suspicion—foresight)…

—*get* **blacklace** *down* (—my wife. *my* love. …), 'n' *cover*. … ("*heroics*"…

hmm. …).

…

—emerges. 'n'… *hovers* (again).

…

a woman emerges (young, early thirts, perhaps).—glasses.

—and *joins him*. …

—chat-chatting (—casual).

and *walk away*. …

…

—and *relax*. … (—relaxation-*release* (o' nervs pent). …).

…

strange.

—to become (to… entertain, and to (part-*wilfully*) exaggerate) suspicion (-suspicious). …

—on the evidence of no more than a seeming display of social awkwardness (a—*not really knowing what to do with oneself*. …),… —*waiting for the woman with th' glasses*. …

—of the same sort 'n' variety that I, myself, displayed—mere moments-minutes afore… —*waiting*—for **blacklace**,—and, half-sarcastically, browsing *lip-stick* shades outside the (open. fronted) cosmetics store–stand. …
(—did anyone *see me* (in that way)… —?).

and that that suspicion (—paranoid-paranoiac *excitation*) should be so easily (-readily) *assuaged* by the presence (appearance-appears) of the young woman (with th' glasses).

…

—all kinds of involunt-(only *semi*-consc., semi-controlled-*mastered*), media (—*news* media), 'n' pop-culture inspired, 'n' (apparently,—at least at first) *uncritical* fears 'n' prejudices (—a heightened state, suspense, of prepared paranoid-paranoiac fear) going on in there. …

UMBRELLA
(—memory of a fragment of-from a dream).

in a café. …
(small-cramped. lit, bright light-lit—pale walls (cream), and large, open, windows.

tea steamed (slight). …).

down.—beside the Piccolo. Teatro. (—the Studio Melato).

…

—to escape (—in-during-through) a (brief,—strong, warm, heavy-fat-sluggish (greasy slight)) rain… *shower*.

…

—the people, (Milanese). sat. beneath the awnings (outside-outwith). …
(—young blonde woman. the table at the end (of the row).—no make-up (nature). pure, crystal, blue eyes.

—striking. beautiful. …).

and the street shills. …

—out. im-mediately. (small, slightly overweight man.—very dark skinned. …).

—to sell umbrellas. …
(—smart, thin-elegant executive (suit) woman… —long, straight, light brown hair…)—purchases-buys—and shelters (with middle-aged, executive man (—sharp-jawed (rugged). suits. short, silver-grey (neat-cropped) hair. …

—her partner? …
(laughing-smiled, perplexed (embarrassed?) at-by the sudden
caught in-by the rain. …).

...

and—*remember*.

…

… —in the ocean-*sea* (—?) (—the shallows). (—broad (long)
beach-coast (stretch 'v).—rocks-cliff over. dark. raining. …).

…

and she says… —*over there.—get the um-* ...
(—*ah, (...)—yes.—the **golf** umbrella*).

…

—across the street (grey (light) paving stones.—concrete),—at the
edge of the water.—the golf umbrella lies-sits on the ground
(opened, large).

(stop. … —might blow away). …

… —fragment of a memory in-of-from a dream.

in the morning.
(Florence).

—in the café (—*RIVOIRE*),—in-on the Piazza Della Signoria. …

… —(on) the last day (morning) in Florence. …

…

—the sun.—comes out (from behind, scant, grey clouds).—above,
-*behind*, the Torre (opposite). …

…

and *dive* (so to.—seeming). … —headlong (felt). for a short while.
… —into the rich (bright) neon(-seeming) orange-pink-
violet(purple) in the eyes (behind the eyelids).

…

"And we tested … " (—line from a poem).
(in-from a dream).

sat with her.

on the couch. (by the windows (bay)).

living room.

(fr'm (as) child(hood). … —bright (light-lit) (natural).—*open*. …).

look over to (at) her.
(… … beautiful.—her face (pale). (eyes. blue).—the long, dark hair…).

—writing. in her notebook (thick). (concentrat-absorb).
(large writing(-hand).—in black-blue, green, and in *red* ink. (volum). …).

smile. (feel).

… —happy. just to be here with her. …

tilt head back. (back (low)-arm (—th' crook), 'v the sofa).
(… —see the leaves 'v trees (red, brown, yellow—autumn), in-through the windows, f'r a moment. …).

…

—has written a poem.
(wants to read.—to-for me. …).

—"*on the Ponte Vecchio*" (Flor)
…

and reads
(… —picture (see)—the bridge.—*Italian* city. (neo-class—th'
buildings (tall), on either.—the water. … bright (sun) light (lit). …
).

—will I get the *joke*… —? …

" ---- --- . .. --- ---- ---
  -- . .. . ------ ---- -- ---
  ------ -- ---- . . . .. --- --
  ---- -- --- - -- ---- . -- .
And we tested every strip of the bed.
  ---- --- ----- . .. --- . ---- "

…

—I *like* that. …

… —"We tested every strip of the bed." … (—*we* tested. …).

(… —the absorb in love. … —the… thoroughness-fastid
(rigorous-exact)—in-'v the lovemaking. …).

"You're free" …
(—near the Hotel.—Ghent. …).

… (… —same street as (on) the Hotel, now. … (—narrow. …
grey. (—dull sky-day). … —office blocks-apart.s. …).

…

strange. …

—*up*. …
(look).

… —a… *figure-ine*.

… (—?). …

(… —*over*-on that… … —*portico* (?—an-the *entrance*…)
(… —grey-municip. …) (—angles-*lines*). …).

—porcelain(?)-*china*—? …

… —'v a *lady*. … in a larg-elaborat pink skirt-dress, … hat-
bonneted…

—carries a placard. (*sign*). …

—"You're free to do AS WE TELL YOU" …

"KNOCKING AROUND HOLLYWOOD."
(—fragments of-from a *strangely intense* dream. …).

(—on the eve of travelling to Cyprus).

…

—roads.-*motorways*.
(broad-wide.—dull, *grey* (intimidate (slight)-*size*. …).—lots 'v
lanes—in'v every-each (both) directions.—through country(side)
(wild hedges,… —fields (behind fences-(grey) crash-
barriers…),… —neat mown (lush green) grass (hills-undulat)
asides. …)).

…

along (walk)-by the side of the road-torway. … —(*sarcastic*)—
think about politics…

… (hear-say) "there is no special deal" (—Blair (was).—on
Brown. …)… —then, of course, there *was* a special deal. …

…

cross over (the motorway (lanes)).

away (now, then)—from roads. … —up a hill (in-cline). (—
country side).

—(tall) unmown grass(es).—beside path (neat.—mown-worn). …

—crumbling walls (—drystone).

…

—they're waiting for me (—*he*'s there,—behind wall,—in a field. (off the path))… —by pre-arrange. …

(… ?)

—(Italy—? —Rome? —Edinburgh (*Pleasance* (corner of—at-with th' Royal Mile). …). …

walking. with *blacklace*. … by (b'side) the (—*huge*,—concrete (grey,—angles (sharp), (clean) glass (fronted)) hotel.

we're going to make love… (—back.—in th' room). …

—"Why don't you go for a walk first (before)?" …

…

… —tall (long high-steep) flight (path) of steps (stairs). … —a (back) street. (narrow. behind.—a *mews* (?) …),—small shop fronts, and backs of tall buildings (Royal Mile). (all Edinburgh stone).

walk down.

…

—hills. (see).—opposite (—over). …

—*green* undulat. (rolling *rise*). (neat grass).

—houses (cluster—*clustered*. …). (small – distant. red. (brick). … —in th' distance (over) fr'm here. …).

short steps (steep),—*jarring* (slight) drop (strain). …

48

…

—*lucky* t' be able to see (have the sight. here). … —all *flat* where
I'm from (no hills. like this).
(-what would she think—looking… —? …).

(… ?)

dress shirt, and tie, but no jacket. …

—at the junction (of the Royal Mile)—town (—*I've seen before*
…).—out.—in the middle of nowhere (down country roads). …).
…

—girl is there. (with others).
(—with a boy. … … —'ll break his heart (when he finds out).
she's definitely with another. …).

(see.—make eye contact).

…

—see her across (the girl)—table (crowded). (with those others
(—many)…).

—ask her (—*mime*)… —"Are you okay?" …

(… ?)

on stage. (back stage).

… —a (*rising*) platform. (large). (stage black.—bare. … —low
light. …).

...

—the vampire,—lying with his lover. (billowing white shirt, long black hair).
(see the stage hand.

—over (above). (on) the lighting rig (platform-a scaffold)).

...

(—?).

(... ?)

HOLLYWOOD agent's office.
(large.—expensive. *gawdy* (tack) decorat. (no taste). ...
—large 80s furniture (dark, grey). *gold* (trim. plated). ...).

with the others.

...

—paternity(suit) 'v a friend. ... —here to establish. ... Doctor. ...

...

—"knocking around Hollywood."
(—was driven. (through-around the hills).—a large (a luxury) car. ...).

(—***must*** *write this down.* ...).

—"You want *anything*,—Just ask. ... "

(—agent. ... —large (broad). middle-aged. balding (black hair. round *pate*). sharp nose. small, round glasses. ... ... —leans in— over table (desk). ...).
(food.—in th' mini-fridge-bar. ... (—bags 'v fruit (pre-cut) (apples—slices), sandwiches,—soft drinks, ...)).

—see telephone note-pad, and (ball point) pen, near (—used).

—try (surreptish) t' steal. ...

...

—Doc.-agent,—describing establishing paternity. (—genetic.— genes. (... —images. up.—'v strands 'v. (—balls. linked.—in chains). ...)).

—the process.

will let us watch.
(—can't share-give *details*.—private. Doctor – patient conf. ...).

...

[TOM CRUISE] arrives. (—outside the off.—a crowded—hall- lobby. (grand.—marble and gold. ostent).)).

—in vamp (eye) make-up. (heavy).—smart black suit. (—a character. ... —?).

... —believes *he* is the father. ...

[KATIE HOLMES] (—dramatic make-up.—short (tight) plastic(?) gold (80s) dress).

...

(—"… fair play to them for turning up, and being involved in-with this production." …).

…

—*take* the notepad (used.—see outlines 'n' pen-lines 'v old (gone) writing…) and pen—fr'm the nearby table (telephone) (by the wall.—gold, 'n' patterned marble—topped. …). …

—must write this down.—for a fragment.
(… don't—*musn't*—*lose.* …).

…

Pokestops—VACUUM.
(—in Nicosia).

in a backstreet. …

—down be-aside the Archbishop's Palace. …

…

...

(*strange*. ... —the work your mind does-work done in the mind (sic. ?),—to resolve-in *resolving*, strange, messy *shapes* seen (—encountered) into sharp, clear, (obvious?) intelligible *signs* (*geometric*)... which *break down* (again) in the recording, whilst *retaining*, somehow, their-that meaning. ...).

THE FEELINGS OF A CHAIR
(Nicosia).

a sign. (seen). …

—on a door(way). …

TO EXPRESS THE FEELINGS OF A CHAIR WHEN WE SIT
ON IT.

… —

…

FUCK YOU Wub DOLFINS
(—the next would-be artist. …)

seen.

(… —the back streets. … in-'v-around the ancient, pedestrian
quarter. …).

(out 'n' about—around—in(-around) Nicosia. …).

(in.—a back street. …).

…

—*FUCK YOU Wub DOLFINS.* …

…

(*hmm*). …

and so,… —searched. (later). …

—to find out *why*—"FUCK YOU," to these… "*Wub –
DOLFINS.*" …

… that, in fact, (—*of course*… —?) refers-referred to a *thread*, …
—on a site called *drawception* (.com), where (on-in which)
someone suggests a theme-topic, which the next personage
through must then *draw*,—the next person along then must *guess*,
as best as can, (then), from this image at what was, at first,
suggested, posting that guess as the suggestion for the next image
of-for the next would-be artist**… …**

… —and this image grew (so to), from a post suggesting "DOLPHINS," which (after an initial image) became, in-within the *guess*, "Dolphins with pig's noses, saying: 'wub wub'." … which, subsequent-in turn, became (become) a *meme*. (of course). …

(—image. … —grows-spawns from arbitrary words suggested,… —words grow (again, in turn, then) from suggestion in-of arbitrary image—interpreted, … give rise (suggest) new(-next) image. … …

—artwork grows-emerges from the slide away, back down, from initial context of artistic inspiration… —away from meaning. … —away, down, … —into (in-to) (the) absurd. …

through the poverty of the artist (to translate-render), and the poverty of language (to capture).

…

—Fuck you, Wub DOLFINS.

…).

(—in a back street. in Nicosia).

…

TREVI.—abstracts. …

the Trevi (Fountain).

(the hotel (this time.—this trip's not far fr'm). …

and, almost strangely,… continue t'… *gravitat* around-t'ward,—
keep *returning* —emerging.—in-to the Piazza (Trevi). in-for-from
every turn (seeming),—'v every *wander*. …).

(and *C.* said, … —on the first visit t' there (this time)… —'pon
arriving (in Rome)… —the hotel. the theatre. … —the pizzeria(-
café) (b'side the theatre),… —the gelateria (by th' fountain)…

—we'll have to come back(-return), at night (-the dark), to take
obligatory, obnoxious, tour-ist shots. …).

…

(—gelato.

…

—the young, English (obnoxious, over-privileged) lad,
continuously shouting… —"KEVIN! KE-VIN! … —Hey,—KE-
VINN!…" …

… … —young couple. kissing.—by the fountain's-side (edge),
(—bottle 'v champagne,—flute-chute glasses. …), and she—lit a
(solitary, small) candle, on a cupcake, and sang "Happy
Birthday!" (in Italian).
(… —applauding, … —wishing "Happy Birthday" with all the
others 'v the crowd(s), gathered. …).).

…

… —managed to take some poor, low-quality (camera-phone) shots-images, that, somehow, (—precisely *because* poor-low-quality… —?) *became*(-h've become), strangely, quite nice (— *effective*) *abstracts*. (—*shapes*. and (in-of) the *light*). …

of night.—around the fountain.

...

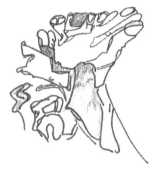

...

...

THE ETHICS OF LITTLE RED RIDING HOOD
(—the *curatore*)
...

(at the *Teatro*,—Rome. ...).

...

before the show.
(*blacklace's*). ...

(—#*DEATHOFGOD*. ... —ol' Shakes's *As You Like It*, ... —
transposed (in-)to a dystopian future state(-world)... —of
manipulated (manipulative) social media, & live-streaming, to-th'-
death gladiatorial com-bat. ... between machine-gun wieldin'
youth "tributes".

...).

—café(space). (drinks). (... —*rich*(-sharp), but... smooth,... light
(*earthy*, grainy... *round* bitter) 'v coffee. ...). (—*long*,... —*white*
(*light*-open, clean),—narrow space. coffee 'n' sandwiches (deli-).

... —chairs, 'n' tables,—in an **L** (—an ■), 'round the long,
large(-broad) counter 'n' prep area. ... smart, vegan-hipster place
vibe. ...).

... —beau-tiful (photo-)realist art(works)-oils on the walls. ... —
gritty(-dirt) urban (tunnel) spaces... —*corners* only (aspects.—
details) of. ... —become dark, geometric abstracts.

...

—a... discussion planned. ... (—*blacklace* ... —sent an invite(-
invited)(—over social media) to attend—t' hear herself speak. ...
(—?)...).

Volante. ...
(—tensed-intense (that... frenetic(? sic)-*passion* (in-tensed) inner-energet (she always) (... —b'hind the eyes... —in-within (focus) movements. ... (—Italian). ...

—talented (seen), *accomplished*, and famous actor. ... —trained with some of the greats 'v European, and 'v Russian modern-contemporary theatre. ...

... —remember. ... watching her.—in rehearsals—'v-for the play (th' show),... and some 'v th'-*her* decisions-directions (—the choices)... were hard to follow-understand... until I saw it (full)—*in the space* (—the *Teatro*,—Milan. ...), and *all* (—the decisions-the directions) *became* (absolutely) *clear*... (—*realised*)... —a (true) *visionary*. (—possessed 'v a *vision* ('v what's t' be). ...).

—the director.

...

—there ('v a sudden)... —fr'm behind that pillar. ... (—the *white* (clean-sharp-edged), (deep) black (-trimmed), smart, art-deco entrance way (-*hall*). ...).

...

—the... "discussion" (-mooted), she says. ... —a *workshop*, then, in fact.

—for the teachers—'v the students who will come to watch the show (play).

and have five minutes (now) (*Christ*)—t' write-prepare (—t' put together). ...
(*blacklace*.—unmoved. ...

and writes (begins to write (out),—in a notebook) a *plan*. (in thirty seconds).

—for exercises (t' perform). ...).

Volante. ... (says)—an exercise.—on staging *perspective* (*hmm*... interest), and the ethics in-of storytelling (the telling 'v a story).

—something like, (on) **RED RIDING HOOD**. ...

...

in the thee-ay-tah's—the *black – box* space.

...

a small group, 'v nine (—five teachers).
(... —ranged 'round th' (audience's) seats-ing,... —with *b* 'n' *V* ... *on stage* (so to)... —seated, at a table. ...).

Volante. ... —long, fluent (Italian—musical elegance), (frankly) *masterful*, (semi-)extempore pre-amble (in-tro).

...

—THE *ROLE* OF THE CHORUS.

...

—*perspective*.

...

blacklace. (—in part- Italian,—part in Eng. ...).

—discusses play…

—the figures (key),… and-*as*—the "chorus."

…

and me.

(—as *curatore del materiale didattico* (—the Curator.—of educational material. (for #*DEATHOFGOD*. …).).

…

—on Nietzsche (ol' Fritz) (—any excuse),… —*The Birth of Tragedy* …

—the chorus (in Greek tragedy(-ies)). … —'s more than, for Nietzsche, a (simple) *exposition*, or… frame-ing (device). …

—(instead,) t' *break down* the… boundaries (or barriers) (so to) 'v the everyday—for-the-audience, and to break down the barrier(s) beween… the world (—the reality) 'v the everyday-the audience, and that (the world) on-of the stage. …

—*immersion* (complete), then, in the world (space-states), and—most important—the *stakes*—the *responsibility* (ethical—for the action)—'v the play (-the stage).

…

an exercise. (physical). (—*Volante* leads). …

—up. in(-as) a group.

(in) a circle. (stand).

...

—count to seven.—hand to shoulder (—*point*),—in the direction you want the count to continue. (to go-t' move).—automatically shifts-changes (in direction) on the count of "*seven*". (—round 'n' round, 'til shifts direction, 'n' round 'n' round. ...).

—to (a) *warm up*.

...

then. (now). ...

—staging "**RED RIDING HOOD.**" ...

...

—a *tableau*.
(t' create).

...

take on roles. (—Red Riding Hood, the Mother, the Grand Mother, the Hunter... —the Wolf. ...).

—take up (fixed) positions-*atttiudes*.
(—the chap as the Wolf... —*magnificent*. (in the... "*spirit*," 'n' the *energy*, 'v the thing. ...).

...

—*blacklace* and I... —the woods.
...

—*I am a tree.*

...

responsibility.

— ... a question of *perspective*.
(—from whose *point of view*. ...). ...

... —how does changing our focus on from whose point of view
the story is being told, *alter* (fundamentally) how we read the
story, and view (, then,) its characters-agents... —? ...

... —the *negligence* (—?) (—who lets her young daughter
venture-walk out, into-through the woods,—*alone*)... —? ... —
itself (, perhaps,) the result (results) of-from the poverty of her
own upbringing at the hands of her own (the Grand-)mother. ... —
?
(—the Wolf a *victim*. ... —? ... —of the woods' failure to *hide*(-t'
shelter) him,... —of the Hunter,... —of Red Riding Hood... —?)

—*responsibility* of-*in*-for the... *situation* in-'v the text... —its
stakes... —?

...

what, then, can ever, truly (—finally) be *known* in-of (the ethics
of) a story?
(what is the *truth*? ... —what *facts* are undeniable—concrete-
incontrovert—*known*. ... —? ...).

—who (, finally,) bears *responsibility*.

... —?

THE BLACK DOG
(—strange night)

...

really... *strange*... *vibe* in the city—night. (... —one of those...
'*cool* (—clear, ... open, ... *airy*) city nights, with a (... —underlaid-
surrounded)... (atmospheric) low... buzz(-hum) (background), of
the excited (anticipat), opening-up, movement-buzz-thrum of
(city) people (moving. out). ... (air—*cool*,... metallic, dust (fume.
exhaust) smelling-*tastes*. slight... *electric*). ...).

—slightly... *acid*,-tense (short-tempered). ...

—tetchy. (hostile?—slight).

...

wander. through tensed (—*flowing*. (narrow-channelled)) crowds.
off the main road-streets, and (*down*—), out-through the
(narrower) back streets (cobbled.—lamp lit).

away fr'm the bright(er), open (rush-busy-ness) 'v the *main –
drag*. (open t' the sky). ...

looking (idle-slight). for dinner-meal. (somewhere).

...

down. (now).—near (to) the PANTHEON.
(—... out.—fr'm side(-rear) street. ...

—*there it is*. (there).

strange.—t' see (it). from this angle. ...

round.

red (thin) bricked. ('v side).
(—orange-grey 'v (street) light(s). 'n' white (bright)—'v *L-E-Ds*
(—?)...).

—*the roof* (vault)-dome(d). ...

... —*incredible structure. ...*).

—out. into (*open*)—be-fountained.—the *Pi-azza.* (cool (air).
night.—*buzz* (obnoxious.-nerv. ...).
(*heavy hiss. ...*

... —vault-arch, columned. 'v the PANTHEON. over. ...).

...

—*and...* yes.—*restaurant touts.* (—bloody dozens). ... —
aggressive(-ly)... *hos-pitable. ...* (—try t' force).

...

—woman there. (—smart-sharp. elegant. suit. (white (shirt). dark
tie. waist-coated). smart-neat uniformed).

—*A table?—This way* ... (Christ.—was only looking (glanced) at
the menu. (brief).—move on. ...).

cross the Piazza's. (corner-edge).

man. (a tout. 'nother).—t' me, and to *blacklace. ...* —
"*Gentleman!*— ... " (—? hmm...).

along—. …

...

...

—down.

—a side street (in-on). (—'way fr'm the Piazza now. … —narrow (white paint-wash,—cobbleds…).

…

—*set back.*

—unimposing. (quiet.—not like the others—all brash—pushy)).

—a restaurant's front.

…

—**THE BLACK DOG**.

...

(?)... —yeah,... —*go on.* ... (quiet-unassume... —*sways.* ...).

small(-ish). (one room). few tables. (round the edges-walls. tables, cloths. (and glasses)). low-warm lit. cheap. (slight) cliché "Italian" (village) fresco-murals on the walls.

empty. (no one. (else-other).—Oh. Aah ...).

Per due—? ...

lady. blonde (-greying) (bob).—gaunt-thin features. (aging). (slight... severe-stern looking—? ... —looks... nonplussed? that someone entered-custom(ers) (at all)...).

Si. ... —points (—gestures-awkward) to table.—(right) at the back. (there).
(*hmm*).

man. (... —stocky-heavy-built. middle-aged—grey(ing), salt 'n' pepper hair (*buzzed*). ... more like a... bouncer, or crime-lord-don, than a restaurater). sits.—at the strange (—*busy-ness* (-like)?—not a till. ... —ignores us entirely. (odd)).

—behind the table (—the back 'v the restaurant). before (front) the kitchen (bright neon-lit (-white tile))—through (—perspex?) window(s) 'v—strange—swing-saloon doors. ...

walk. (okay.—reluctant).

and... —sit. ...

—*str-ange.* ... —"cheesy"(chee-zee), retro (—'80s) "love" soundtrack (plays). (—ee-zee lis-nin' "jaaa-aaaz" (—*sleazes*)). ...

(... *turn*(ing). ... ... —small TV screen. (—incongr- ...).
showing-plays... football(?). by—the window (?... —not a sports
bar. ...).

—browse the menu (then). (awkward.—while she... *hovers*
(there), standing, and he *sits*. ...).
(we. ... —*smile*. ... (t' one another).—surreptitious (try). (am-be-
mused). ...).

... —choose.

—(she) looks irritat. (—by choices?—drinks... —?).

...

strange. ... —movement (she. he. ... —both) (—*far too much*),
back 'n' forth, (and back 'n' forth),... —through th' swinging
doors.
(are they- ?... —are they- cooking it (the food) themselves... —?
...

—some... con-ference... —do they (anyone-anybody back there
(is there?) knows *how* to cook (even)—? ...).

bustle. ... (another) lady (young)... —in (fr'm the street-out),—
kitchen—uniformed (apron), and through t' the kitchen (again)—
without even acknowledge (—staff... ?).

(*hmm*).

fairy lights. (odd).—wrapped around—a *tree*. (—dead?).—a-
beside(-behind) the-our table. ...

• • •

ah. ... (—here). (she)... —the food. (serve).
...

73

food is *bad* (not good)… —pasta undercooked. sauce—*sweet* (slight.-generic).—bland. (—stodge).

…

a man.

walks in (clatter—'v-at door) (overweight (slight) aging(-late) middle-aged (corpul), grey-greying thinning hair. (thick, bush moustache). dark blue suit (light-sky blue shirt. (collar.—open). …).

chats (—Italian). ease-familiar. but slight… gruff (authorit.—no *patience*).

(t') patron-ise.

'n'—*sits*. (—lounges… —casual (almost… obscene(—?)—th' *attitude*-posture. …).

—at table (—for four).—by the wall and window-front. (to watch—the football. …). (—p'rhaps the TV's f'r him (partic)… —?).

—*strange*. … immediate *animation*(-urgence) in th' deskman. …

—moves (sudden).—abandons… … whatever it was he was doing (or,… —eating… —?)—? …). …

—t' *accommodate*.

…

—*strange vibe*. …

—woman and man, rush t' pander.

... —h'd thought *he* (—deskman-don)—in his ill-temper, and indifferent-ignor—'s the *boss* (-th' *owner*). ...

but, ... —rushes over.—t' th' suited other. ...

—'n' sits with—obsee-qu- (*nervous*—?)...
(—a *junior* (sub-ord)?)

—this other, (suit-ed) owns-in charge. (—the *boss*)... —?

...

strange. ...

—wonder... —? ...

—a *front*. ... —? ... —f'r mo-ney launderin'—? (—the **Mob**). ...
—?
(... —explains the... *emptiness* in-'v, and the *bad*,—(the) improv, food. ...).

—?

...

(finished.—as far as can. ...).

—get the bill. ...

...

—pay.

...

—and *leave*. ... —*quickly*.
(*strange*. ...).

the woman in the church

...

beautiful building (striking). church. ...

—set back. fr'm the street('s front). (a-midst (otherwise)...
ordinarily (...) —*Roman* buildings (arch). ...).

—neo-classic archi—statuary-columns-(plinths)—*lines-angles-*...
planes ('n' *sur-faces*) (shadows), and (in) *details.* ... —*symmetry.*
(grand-imposing (height)-ostentate). ...

...

in(-side). ...

(... *cool... smell...*

—*deep*, rich, ... —*old...* —*organic*(?—warm-*stale*)—wood,
(cold... -*round*-hollow), *mineral*-(iron)metallic 'v stone, and bitter
(faint)-acrid (sharp-sour)-*chemical* 'v wood *polish*(ed). ...

—*hm-Aah.* ... —*takes me back.* (say). ... child(hood)-youth—in
the church. ...
(something... (deeply) familiar. (—some... *solid*-grounded, *full*,
definite feeling. (*conservatism 'v memorial*) down in (—always—
still—... —back, down (there))... —space, smell—sensation ('n'
feeling)... 'n'—leaps across the gap, in-between the now-here,
and the then (way back). ... —t' re-ignite (sic)—t' call back that
past, in-to (in-within) the-this-here present. ...).

beautiful. ... rich (abund) elaborate painting-artworks-frescoes.
(saints, 'n' scenes—in-'v-from Heaven (heavens). ...
(—carving (-carvings) stone, ornate, adorn (around). ...).).
...

blacklace. ... —lights two candles (give a Euro€), ... —for her parents.
(stand over here (away). (—discrete-respectful distance (fr'm))...
—give her (the) space,—unless she *needs* you.

...

—these leaflets, DVDs (—life 'v a saint...), and postcards, here (—stand). ...

... —*chapel*. (dedicated)—to a young nun.—died (young)—of tuberculosis. ... (*hmm*. ... —sad. ...).
(—lots 'v (side-)chapels-shrines... —along-line th' walls 'v the church (main.-body-space). ... —all dedicat (seems) t'... *fame-ous* Christian bodies-figures. (strangely... *populist*. ... —?) (with... *odd*.—cheap(-looking) photos-pictures, framed. ...).

...

—a woman.

—not far off (down th'). ...

(—blonde (light-coloured), *styled* hair (*long*—straightened). ...

made-up.

—thin-elegant (body—worked on...) *pointed* (features-face). ...

—aging,... but well-kept (maintained), browned (tanned) olive skin. ...

79

—close fit, long (smooth-flows) black dress, 'n'… accessories-bling-jewellery (large, *gold*) (… heavy (-over?) *styled*. (—too… *young* for her… —?). …).

stands—t' the (a-)side… —next that chapel (—centre). …

…

—man. with a camera. (early middleage.—looks… *casual* (dress.—tee-shirt, jacket, jeans). … —cam'ra looks… professional (—*semi*- …). (—not high spec or *studio*. … —no others—… techies, 'qupiment,… —lighting, make-up, &c. …).).

… .—'nother man. … (younger?—also casual).—with a camera phone (video) on (-t'ward) her. …

…

(*gesture*. (—nod-point. …).—t' indicate.—as… subtle(?), as can, please)—t' *blacklace*. (—she hasn't seen-spotted). …

—I think she's going to *sing*.

…

yes. … (sure 'nough.—there it is). …

music.

(…).

—I-talian pop-*soul* (?) (a) *beat*. … —light,—*rolling* instrumental rhythm-melody. …

… —sampled (synth) (male) choral,—religious (Gregori) inf.d
(sampled) *harmonies*. (slightly… —*tinny* (shrill.—aqueous).
(—male, castrato(?)—*La-la – LAH*-s. (…). …).

(she dances (slight).—… gentle (delicat-easy), with her arms-
hands (gentle-simple semi-circs).

—Intro.
…

begins to sing.—to *mime*.

—the voice (on the tape-recording)… —too… *young*. and light. to
be hers.

…

—the music. (slightly tinny recording). …

—being. … —*piped-in* (in-t' the church-space).

(*where*? …).

—there. (yes). … —(fr'm) speakers. on top 'v pillar(-lintels)
(round).
…

strange… gold-coloured-painted (spray) speakers. (more… *holy*,
that way… —?).
…

—each got. … (yes).—(adorned).—little gold plastic cherubs. (—
?).

…

—filming.—a *music vi-deo*. …

IF THE FUTURE NEEDS A COLOUR.
(—BIG BROTHER IS WATCHING). ...

...

there.
(*wall*.—beige-*grey* 'v *con-crete*. (munici-)brutalist (—?). ...).

...

—side street.
(the river.—*Tiber*.—over. ...).
(up. (here). ... —fr'm Trastevere. (... —my favourite part of
Rome, still,—I think. ... —the neighbourhood (archi – vibe.—
narrow, old-town, streets),—the river (open. air.—the *view*)). ...
—(on) t'ward the Vatican(-Basilica).

(—mid-half (part-)way). ...).

...

(—a sign (? sic). ... —a message-*image*. ...).

—PUTTING HOLES IN HAPPINESS
WE'LL PAINT THE FUTURE BLACK
IF IT NEEDS A COLOR ...

(—BIG BROTHER IS WATCHING YOU.)

...

PUTTING HOLES IN HAPPINESS
WE'LL PAINT THE FUTURE BLACK
IF IT NEEDS A COLOR...

KNIVES

"DEUS!" …

…

there.

…

—th' wall (—a pillar.—flat-*square* (bulk-hulk),—stocky,
brutalist) 'v the (road) tunnel. …

—th' wall (—a pillar.—flat-*square* (bulk-hulk),—stocky,
brutalist) 'v the (road) tunnel. …
(—grey(-beige) rough(-*coarse*) 'v concrete.—(matt) coal-black
dust 'v soot-*grime* (fuel. smoke-fume). air—dust, stained-staining
(rising.—foot (ground) 'v the pillar.—up. (rising.—damp)).).

…

—strange, dull (headache?)… —*orange-grey* 'v (munici)
streetlamps, lights. (—dull, dry *wash*). …

—through th' bus window (dirt 'v)… —sharp-quick, 's passing
(through) (—th' poorer neighbourhoods (ghettos)—on th' way
through.—t' the airport. …).

for a moment.

…

84

DEUS!

...

—the *tag*. ... 'v a graffiti (a street) artist.

... —strange,... *sudden*,... (non-sequit), despairing (an *angered*) cry—t' the Heavens. ...

—for **absolution**.
(... —?).

• • •

Mark Bolsover is a freelance writer, living and working in Edinburgh. He has short experimental prose-poetry published, and forthcoming, in a number of international literary magazines, in print, and online. His piece, 'eye contact (or,... —an only optical love),' was a winner of the Into the Void Poetry Competition (2016). His debut Chapbook, *IN FAILURE & IN RUINS—dreams & fragments*, was published with Into the Void Press (Dublin & Toronto, May 2017).

https://intothevoidmagazine.com/product/in-failure-in-ruins-dreams-fragments-by-mark-bolsover/